CatNips

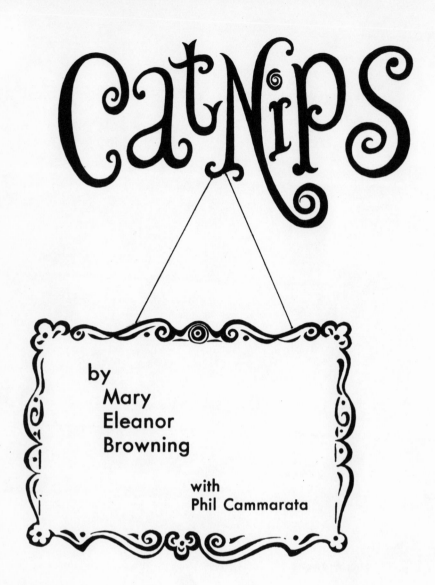

CatNips

by
Mary
Eleanor
Browning

with
Phil Cammarata

PRENTICE-HALL, INC.
Englewood Cliffs, N.J.

Fifth printing.........May, 1965

Printed in the United States of America
12112-T

CatNips

Now **that's** what I call a dry martini!

1

Before we continue on the subject of human behavior,
who's the wiseguy who threw the spitball?

We shall now sing Hymn 3 on page 4.

But, my son is too young to go into the army!

Since you've made your mother and me prospective grandparents
we suggest you get married.

Excuses, excuses, excuses . . .

Let's compose ourselves . . . it's only a poodle.

Don't tell me Helen, let me guess . . . you rapped up the car again.

Is **that** what they mean by abstract art?

Five dollars to win on Lucky Lucy.

Do you mind covering up when you sneeze!

Oh stop carrying on this way . . . he's not the only boy in the world.

Miss Browning . . . I can't hold this pose all day you know.

Are you a preacher or a hotel manager? . . . of course she's my wife.

... And don't try to murder the ball. Just get on base.

What can I do, Doctor? . . . She simply won't eat anything.

Mr. Higgenbottom! And you a Married man!

How else would you scratch your ear?

Nobody loves me.

But, of **course** one wears white gloves to a catnip tea.

Mr. Ferguson, your conduct at the Christmas party was inexcusable.

When I was seven I beat my dolly with a hammer.

You'll hear rumors about me being a vicious, rotten, mean first sergeant . . .
Well they're all a pack of truths.

Darn Hangnail!

I don't know why you children insist on watching these horror shows.

That's the last time I'll put a mushroom in a martini.

Darn! Here comes the rain and I forgot my umbrella.

I'd like to see Chubby Checker try this!

Give me **one** good reason why women shouldn't be in politics.

Aw, c'mon honey, open the door. I didn't mean it . . .

We are **not** Hungarians! . . . and we are **not** sisters!

Gosh, I'm sorry Clarence. It's just that my mother says
we're too **young** to go steady.

It's an unpretentious little wine, but, I think you'll find it interesting.

I swear I saw Brigitte Bardot!

How do you like my new contact lenses?

I was the only fighter who ever had Joe Louis worried.

A haircut is murder without a shower . . .

Don't look now, but I think there's a peeping tom-cat at the window.

She had only one drink . . . would you believe it?

If I wasn't crazy when you married me . . .
you would have driven me nuts any way.

Well, you wouldn't win any beauty contest, but your features are good.

I don't think that was a **bit** funny.

Me frightened? . . . Mister, rockets are my business.

Gregg, I'm afraid it's all over between us.

DO — RE — ME — FA — SO — LA LA LA

Okay, wiseguy! Let's see your license and registration.

Really Mabel, it's a great new way to reduce.
Why, I've already lost ten pounds in ten days.

And why must your mother always come **here**?
That old bat could easily fly to Dracula's house.

It's simple . . . Pretend you're stepping on a cigarette while drying your back with a towel.

You're my husband's new secretary, aren't you?

I can't thread a needle **with** glasses, let alone without them.

The major problem in your marriage is
the inability to communicate your feelings to each other.

Billy, **must** you humiliate me in public?

Take your hands off that dress. I saw it first!

Marge, you wanna' throw down a fresh towel!

Honey, it's two in the morning. Where am I going to get cigarettes at this hour?

And the next time I see you winking at another woman . . .

I usually only have to **sing** for my supper.

Somehow I just don't blend into this environment.

I dunno . . . I guess I'm just in a blue funk today.

Why no, Miss Pinchmire, I have no idea who put that tack on your seat.

Why son, when I was your age . . .

I don't care if the bases **are** loaded, it's your turn to get the beer.

Yeah, but cats can't talk.

If she was just a business associate, why did she hang up when I answered?

Please, Pop, can we keep him? Please?

Look Ma! One foot!

I am **not** wearing an Ivy League hairpiece!

It's really a funny joke, if I can ever get to the punch line.

Don't worry, Lenny . . . Someday we're going to have our own rabbit farm.

My dear doctor, about those pep pills you prescribed for me . . .

8 ball in the side pocket.

And if elected . . .

Wanna' know somethin' Marty? I'm beginnin' to like girls too.

I've got 40,000 transit workers waitin' to strike!!

For the last time — no tickee, no shirtee.

"And now, ladies and gentlemen, the Late, Late Show."

Mrs. Goldberg, remember a month ago when you borrowed my steam iron for just ten minutes?

Hey Baby . . . I'm home on furlough!

The chair recognizes Mrs. Turkeyfeathers, who will tell you
all about our upcoming bazaar.

1-2 cha, cha, cha . . . 3-4 cha, cha, cha . . .

You paid **how** much for that hat!

That, children, is a mouse.

More than anything in the world, I want to be an actress.

My son has told me a great deal about you,
Miss La Rue.

I'm sorry, sir, but it doesn't come off.

I can't believe this will really help my figure.